Let's read and talk about...

Keeping Fit

Honor Head

W

FRANKLIN WATTS
LONDON • SYDNEY

Franklin Watts
338 Euston Road, London NW1 3BH

Franklin Watts Australia
Level 17/207 Kent St, Sydney, NSW 2000

This edition copyright © Franklin Watts 2014

Created by Taglines Creative Ltd: www.taglinescreative.com
Author: Honor Head
Series designer: Hayley Cove
Editor: Jean Coppendale

Fitness consultant: Angeline Westley is a qualified & experienced Fitness & Nutrition Instructor, and the creator of NutriSkill - Food & Health Programmes & Resources provided by Tailored Learning Resources Ltd, of which she is Managing Director.
Series literacy consultant: Kate Ruttle is a freelance literacy consultant and Literacy Co-ordinator, Special Needs Co-ordinator and Deputy Head at a primary school in Suffolk.

ISBN: 978 1 4451 3213 6
Dewey classification: 613.7
A CIP catalogue for this book is available from the British Library.

Picture credits
t=top b=bottom l=left r=right
Cover: Jacek Chabraszewski/Shutterstock.
Series icons: books, Osa; Jut; dddelli/Shutterstock; speech bubbles, Dic Liew/Shutterstock; ball, Sashkin/Shutterstock.
6 Jacek Chabraszewski/Shutterstock; 7 ifoto/Shutterstock; 8 Jules Studio/Shutterstock; 9 Greenland/Shutterstock; 10 Gennadiy Titkov/Shutterstock; 11 Nate A/Shutterstock; 12 Mandy Godbehear/Shutterstock; 13 agefotostock/SuperStock; 14 Jaimie Duplass/Shutterstock; 15t wavebreakmedia ltd/Shutterstock; 15b Serge64/Shutterstock; 16 Olga Lyubkina/Shutterstock;17t Monkey Business Images/Shutterstock; 17b Jacek Chabraszewski/Shutterstock; 18 Gorilla/Shutterstock; 19l Juriah Mosin/Shutterstock; 19r Dean Mitchell/Shutterstock; 20 Joe Gough/Shutterstock; 21, 22, 23 Jacek Chabraszewski/Shutterstock; 24 Robert Pernell/Shutterstock; 25t Milena/Shutterstock; 25b goldenangel/Shutterstock; 26 goran cakmazovic/Shutterstock; 27 Monkey Business Images/Shutterstock.

Every attempt has been made to clear copyright on the photographs used in this book. Should there be any inadvertent omission please apply to the publisher for rectification.

Printed in China

Franklin Watts is a division of Hachette Children's Books, an Hachette UK company.
www.hachette.co.uk

Contents

Pages marked with ⬇ have a free downloadable activity sheet at www.franklinwatts/downloads. Find out more on page 30.

Words in **bold** are in the glossary on page 29.

What is being fit?

Being fit means you have loads of energy. You feel good and your body is working well.

Having the energy to run and play with your friends is all part of being fit.

Why do I need to be fit?

When you are fit you stay healthy, your body grows strong and works properly. You also have more energy to enjoy yourself and do lots of different activities.

Does keeping fit make me feel good?

Yes, keeping fit makes you feel **positive** and gives you more **confidence**. When you exercise, chemicals called **endorphins** are released into your blood stream and these make you feel good.

Will being fit help me at school?

Yes, when you eat well, sleep well and exercise regularly you work better in school. You'll be able to **concentrate** more on your work. You will also have plenty of energy left over after school, as well.

A fit body means your brain works better, too.

Talk about

✪ What do you think being fit means?

✪ Why do you think being fit is good?

✪ Are you as fit as you can be? How could you be fitter?

TAKE ACTION

Keep an exercise diary for a week. Make a note of any exercise you do including walking to school or the shops. Keep this for page 28.

How does keeping fit help my body?

Exercise helps your muscles and bones to grow strong.

How does keeping fit help muscles?

Muscles are attached to your bones and help you to move. The more you use your muscles the bigger and stronger they become. Different activities use and strengthen different sets of muscles.

Will I get huge muscles like weightlifters?
No! Weightlifters do special exercises and use heavy weights every day to build their massive muscles. You should not use weights. Taking part in sports and doing regular exercise will be enough to keep your muscles strong and working well.

Playing games such as tennis will help your arm and leg muscles to stay strong.

How does keeping fit help my bones?

Exercise and a good diet help your bones to grow strong. Exercise also keeps your **joints**, such as your knees and shoulders, **flexible** and moving well.

Talk about

✪ How do you feel after you've exercised?

✪ How would being fitter make you feel better?

Wall climbing helps your bones to grow strong and is great fun.

TAKE ACTION

Fancy learning a new sport? Speak to your local sports centre and find out what's available.

Read about

Is exercise good for my heart and lungs?

Yes, regular exercise keeps your heart and lungs working well.

How does exercise help my heart?

Regular exercise will help to keep your heart strong so that it works properly. Your heart is a muscle that pumps blood around your body. The blood takes **nutrients** from your food and **oxygen** from the air to all parts of your body so it can work well.

When you play games, such as basketball, your heart beats harder and faster.

Why does my heart beat faster when I exercise hard?

Your body needs more oxygen when it is exercising. The faster your heart beats, the more oxygen is carried around your body in your blood.

How does exercise help my lungs?

Exercise such as running or swimming makes you breathe more deeply which strengthens your lungs. Having a stronger heart and lungs mean you can do more exercise without getting breathless and tired.

Talk about

⊗ **Do you ever get out of breath? When?**

⊗ **Why do you get out of breath?**

⊗ **How do you think doing more exercise helps your breathing?**

When you run your heart beats faster and your lungs work harder.

Read about

How does being fit make me feel good?

Being fit makes you feel better about yourself and increases your confidence.

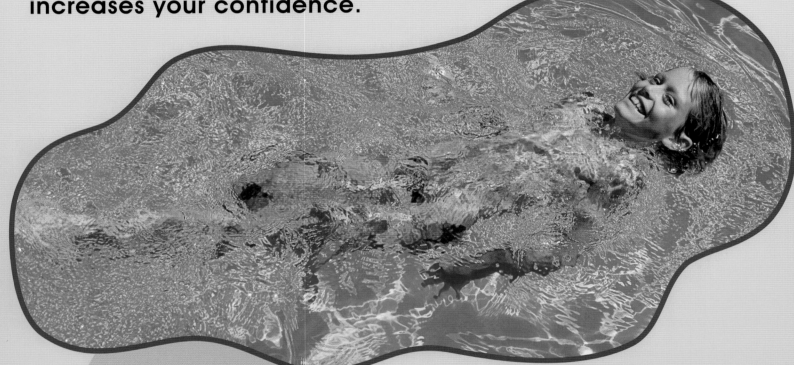

Swimming is a great activity and could save your life.

Why does exercise make me feel good?
If you've been sitting at a desk for a long time you need to stretch your body by running around, playing a game or going for a swim. This will help you to relax and to sleep well.

12

How does exercise increase my confidence?

When you get better and better at a new game or sport this gives your **self-confidence** a boost. It is also a great feeling when you learn a new skill, such as riding a bike, ice skating or skateboarding.

When you are cycling always wear a safety helmet.

Learning to ride a bike is exciting and good exercise.

TAKE ACTION

Get together with friends or family. Choose three new activities you've never tried before. See if you can do these in the next month.

What about team sports?

Playing a team sport helps you to learn how to work with other people. It's also a good way to make new friends. You could join a club – or why not get some friends together to start your own sports team or fitness club?

Talk about

○ What new activites would you like to try?

○ Why do you think some people are scared to try something new?

13

Is being fit the same as being healthy?

Being fit is part of having a healthy lifestyle.

What's a healthy lifestyle?

A healthy lifestyle means doing the right amount of exercise and eating a balanced diet. You also need to get plenty of sleep to help you feel good.

How much sleep do I need?

You need at least 10 hours sleep each night. Sleep gives your body and brain time to rest so that you are on top form for the next day.

TAKE ACTION

Keep a sleep diary. Note how many hours you sleep each night for a week. Is it enough?

A good night's sleep will help you to work better and feel great the next day.

What is a balanced diet?

For a healthy balanced diet you should eat starchy foods such as pasta, rice and bread that contain **carbohydrates**. Also eat some **protein** and **dairy foods** as well as fruit and vegetables every day.

Talk about

✪ How do you feel when you wake up? Do you think you get enough sleep?

✪ How could you make your diet more 'balanced'?

Spaghetti with tomato sauce and salad is a tasty, balanced meal.

Eat at least five **portions** of fruit and vegetables a day as part of your healthy diet.

15

What sort of exercise is best?

All exercise is good – the best exercise is the one you enjoy doing.

Which exercises make me strong?
Most exercise will keep your body fit and help to build up your strength. For strong muscles and **stamina**, try sports such as rowing, cycling and running.

TAKE ACTION

Get two teams together with your friends, family or classmates. Have a mini competition — try running, skipping, hopping or just playing catch.

Rowing and kayaking are good for strengthening arm muscles.

What is aerobic exercise?

Aerobic exercise is any exercise or sport that makes your heart beat faster so that more oxygen is pumped around your body. Aerobic exercise also helps you to get rid of extra body weight. Being **overweight** is bad for your heart, bones and muscles.

Are gymnastics and yoga good exercise?

Yes, because both make you move and stretch your joints and muscles. Gymnastics and **yoga** help keep your body supple and joints working well.

If you do yoga stretches they should be slow and gentle.

Skipping is an aerobic exercise and makes your heart beat faster.

Talk about

✪ What sort of exercise do you enjoy doing?

✪ How do you think this could help you to stay fit?

17

How much exercise should I do?

Try to do at least 60 minutes exercise a day including weekends.

Does it matter what exercise I do?
Doing a mix of activities is best as this stops you from getting bored and uses different parts of your body. It's good to try some exercises outdoors and indoors.

TAKE ACTION

Get two groups together and each invent a new ball game. Which one is best?

Sledging is fun and a good outdoors activity when it is snowy.

What if I don't have enough time?

You don't have to do 60 minutes in one go!
Try to fit some exercise into your daily routine.
Walk to school or to visit friends or family. Use
the stairs instead of a lift or escalator.

Washing the car counts as part of your keeping fit plan.

Talk about

✪ How can you make more time to get active?

✪ How could you fit more exercise into your daily routine?

Can I exercise too much in one go?

Yes, especially if you are just starting. Try to
do a little each day and do more as you
get fitter. If you feel dizzy or sick stop and
rest. Make sure you warm up and cool
down properly (see page 22).

A walk in the park with your family is a great way to exercise together.

Read about

Do some foods give me energy?

You need to eat enough of the right kind of food to give you the energy you need for exercising and to keep you fit.

Which foods give me energy?

Carbohydrates in foods such as pasta, rice, potatoes and bread are good for energy and you should try to eat one of these at every meal. Don't eat a big meal or snack before an activity, and don't exercise for about two hours after a meal.

Pasta contains carbohydrates that help to give you energy.

What are good high-energy snacks?

For a quick high energy snack try a skimmed milk smoothie, low-fat yogurt, a handful of mixed nuts or a piece of fruit such as a banana or apple. Even if you are exercising a lot, try not to eat too many sweets, pies, crisps or pastries. Keep these as **treats**.

Talk about

✪ **What are the best kinds of food to eat if you are exercising regularly?**

✪ **Discuss what a healthy menu for a day might be.**

The best drink when you're exercising is plain water.

Do I have to drink lots of water?

Yes, when you exercise you get hot and sweat. This is your body's way of keeping cool. You need to replace the water you lose when you sweat, so you should drink more.

What is warming up and cooling down?

These are activities you should do before and after you exercise.

Why do I need to warm up?

When you exercise you tighten and shorten your muscles. Warming up helps to prepare your muscles for activity. If you don't warm up, you could damage your muscles. Warming up also increases your **heart rate** slowly and safely.

Even if you're playing football in the park, warm up before you start a game.

How do I warm up?

To warm up safely you should begin by jogging on the spot or running around gently for about five minutes. When you feel nicely warm do some gentle stretches.

Which stretches are best?

When you stretch do it slowly. Don't twist or turn too quickly as this might make your muscles sore. Touch your toes and gently stretch your arms above your head.

Bend one leg and stretch the other behind you to warm up your leg muscles.

Talk about

✪ **Why do you think it's important to get your body ready for exercise?**

✪ **What gentle stretching exercises can you think of?**

Why do I need to cool down?

If you stop exercising suddenly and flop into the car or a chair, you might feel light-headed or dizzy. You need to let your heart rate slow down gently. Do some slow stretches or walk around until your breathing and heartbeat are back to normal.

Do I need special clothes and shoes?

It depends on what you do. You need to keep safe and feel comfortable.

Are shoes important?

Yes, they are. When you run or skip your feet hit the ground hard and this can damage your bones and joints. Kicking a football around can damage your toes.

Football boots with studs help to stop you slipping and protect your feet and toes.

So what shoes are best?

If you are running around it's best to wear trainers that have a thick sole. These will help to make sure your leg and foot joints and bones are protected.

What about safety clothes?

If you go cycling you should always wear a safety helmet. For skateboarding you need to protect your head and joints. If you are going out after dark, wear something with a bright stripe that shines in the dark.

Trainers have special thick soles

Skateboarding is exciting but make sure you wear the right safety gear.

Talk about

✪ Why is it a good thing to wear the right clothes when exercising?

✪ How else can you keep safe while you are exercising?

25

How do I get started?

Begin today. Look for a local exercise class or start your own group.

Where can I find local groups?
Look online, in your local paper, ask friends or ask at your local sports centre. They may have classes such as martial arts, netball or badminton. Ask your sports teacher about any after-school activities you could join.

TAKE ACTION
Decide today how you can do more exercise — it could be walking to school, dancing for 20 minutes at home or joining a sports group or club.

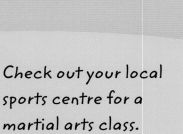
Check out your local sports centre for a martial arts class.

Can I start my own group?

Great idea! Get a few friends together to meet three times a week at the park or someone's house for sports or games. Give your group a name.

Meet up with your friends in the park and plan your activities for the week.

Talk about

✪ **Think about the type of activity you would like to do – would it be a team sport, something with just you and your best friend or do you prefer to exercise alone?**

What about when it rains?

Have fun thinking of indoor games you can do. Play **mirrors** or use a balloon as a volleyball. Or how about surprising the grown-ups by offering to do the dusting or hoovering!

Talk about

❂ Check out your exercise diary (see page 7). Are you doing enough different types of exercise each day?

❂ How can being fit help you at school?

❂ Think about your lifestyle. Do you think it's healthy? Could it be better? How could you make it better?

❂ What local activities are there that would help to keep you fit? Is there a local park, swimming pool or bicycle path?

❂ Being fit means your heart and lungs work well. What else does being fit mean?

❂ What sort of fun exercises or activities could you do with your friends?

Glossary

carbohydrates the part of your food that gives you energy

concentrate to focus on what you're doing and not feel fidgety or tired

confidence when you feel good about yourself, what you do and the way you look

dairy foods a food group that includes milk, cheese and yogurt

endorphins chemicals that are released into your blood when you exercise. They are called the 'feel good' chemicals because after exercise many people say they feel happy and full of energy

flexible when your joints are working well and are not stiff so that you can bend and stretch your body without feeling any pain or strain

heart rate how fast your heart beats

joints parts of your body that hold two bones together and allow you to move, such as your knees and your elbows

mirrors a game where two people stand facing each other. One person makes lots of moves which the 'mirror' has to copy

nutrients the good bits of your food that help your body to stay healthy

overweight when your body is storing too much fat. We use energy from our food when we move. If we eat a lot and don't move enough, this energy is stored as fat

oxygen a colourless gas that is all around us that we need to live. You breathe in oxygen and it travels around your body in your bloodstream

portions the amount of food you eat. The size of a portion depends on the type of food you are eating, your age and size

positive feeling good and upbeat

protein part of the food that we eat that helps us to grow muscles and stay healthy

self-confidence feeling good about yourself and that you are able to have a go at most things

stamina when you are able to stay active for longer without feeling tired or getting out of breath

treats something special to have every now and again but not every day

yoga a form of exercise that makes you stretch your body

Index

Activity sheets

The following spreads have accompanying worksheets, which are available to download for free at www.franklinwatts.co.uk

What is being fit? (pages 6–7)
A handy sheet for keeping a record of the exercise you have done in a week.

How does being fit make me feel good? (pages 12–13)
Use this writing frame to explain how exercise makes you feel.

How do I get started? (pages 26–27)
A poster summarising the benefits of keeping fit.